FRUIT ON THE BEACH
PHOTOGRAPHS BY DON RIEPE

JAMAICA BAY PAMPHLET LIBRARY 05

FRUIT ON THE BEACH
PHOTOGRAPHS BY DON RIEPE

STRUCTURES OF COASTAL RESILIENCE
Jamaica Bay Team
Spitzer School of Architecture
The City College of New York

Catherine Seavitt Nordenson, editor
Associate Professor of Landscape Architecture

Kjirsten Alexander
Research Associate

Danae Alessi
Research Associate

Eli Sands
Research Assistant

JAMAICA BAY PAMPHLET LIBRARY
05 Fruit on the Beach
Photographs by Don Riepe

ISBN 978-1-942900-05-4

COPYRIGHT

CONTACT

Catherine Seavitt Nordenson
cseavittnordenson@ccny.cuny.edu
www.structuresofcoastalresilience.org

SCR Jamaica Bay Team
The City College of New York
Spitzer School of Architecture
Program in Landscape Architecture, Room 2M24A
141 Convent Avenue New York, New York 10031

COVER

Canada goose eating banana.
photo: Don Riepe

supported by

THE ROCKEFELLER FOUNDATION

SCR
Structures of Coastal Resilience

CUNY
The City University of New York

The City College of New York

6

Tern and DiamondbackTerrapin Nesting area, Jamaica Bay Wildlife Refuge, West Pond, looking east. c. 1984

Jamaica Bay Wildlife Refuge, West Pond Trail, looking east. c. 1984

Rituals at North Channel Beach parking lot, looking north. c. 1998

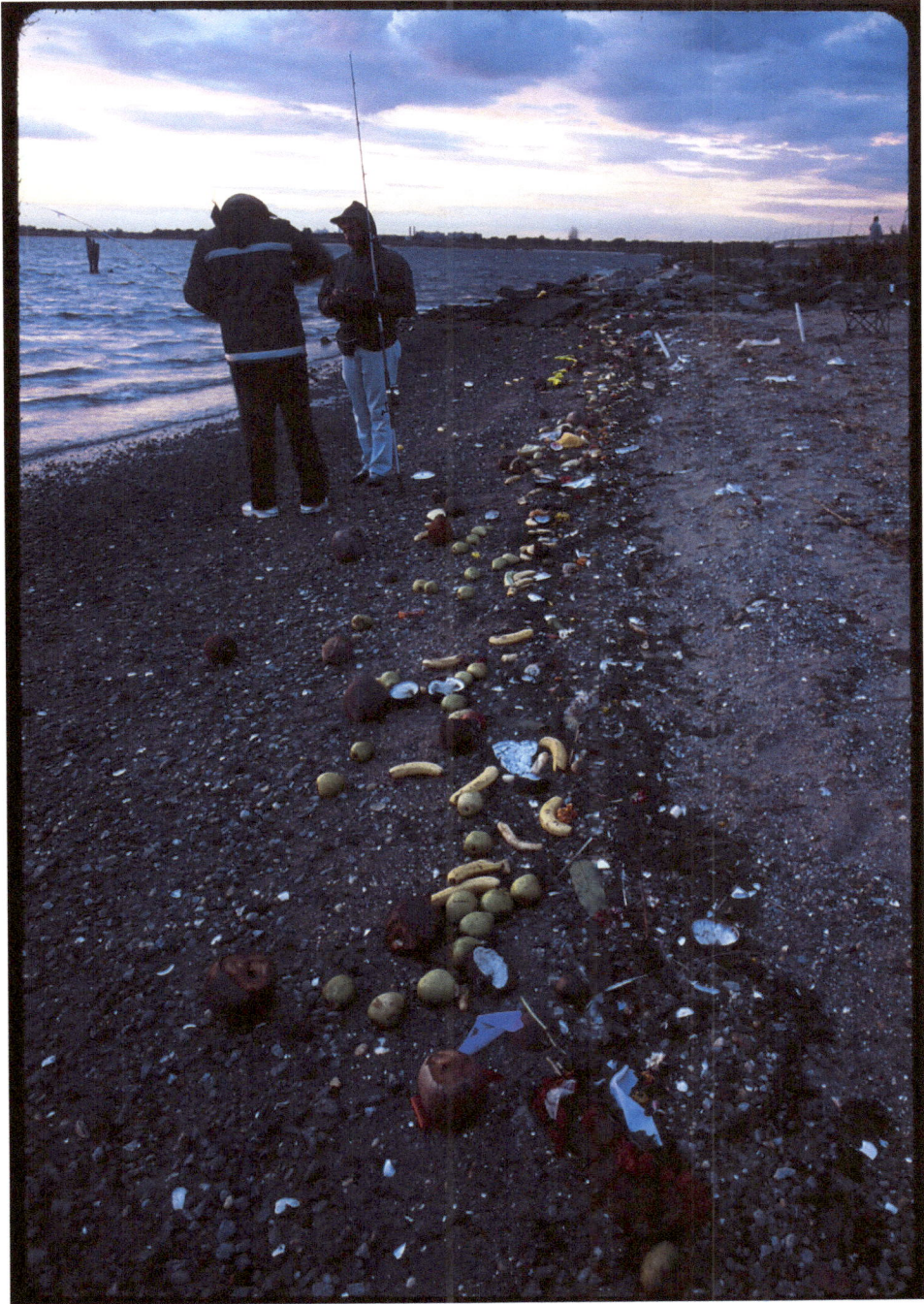

Fruit on the beach. c. 1998

JoCo Marsh and JFK runway, looking north-east. 1994

Osprey platform and JFK Airport, looking north-east. 1994

Jamaica Bay Wildlife Refuge Visitor Center (prior to reconstruction), looking north-west. c. 1970

Cross Bay Boulevard, Broad Channel and East Pond, looking north. c. 1986

Old bulkhead, Dubos Point, original "Buffer the Bay" parkland acquisition. c. 1994

Old bulkhead, Vernam Basin / "Lost Point." c. 1987

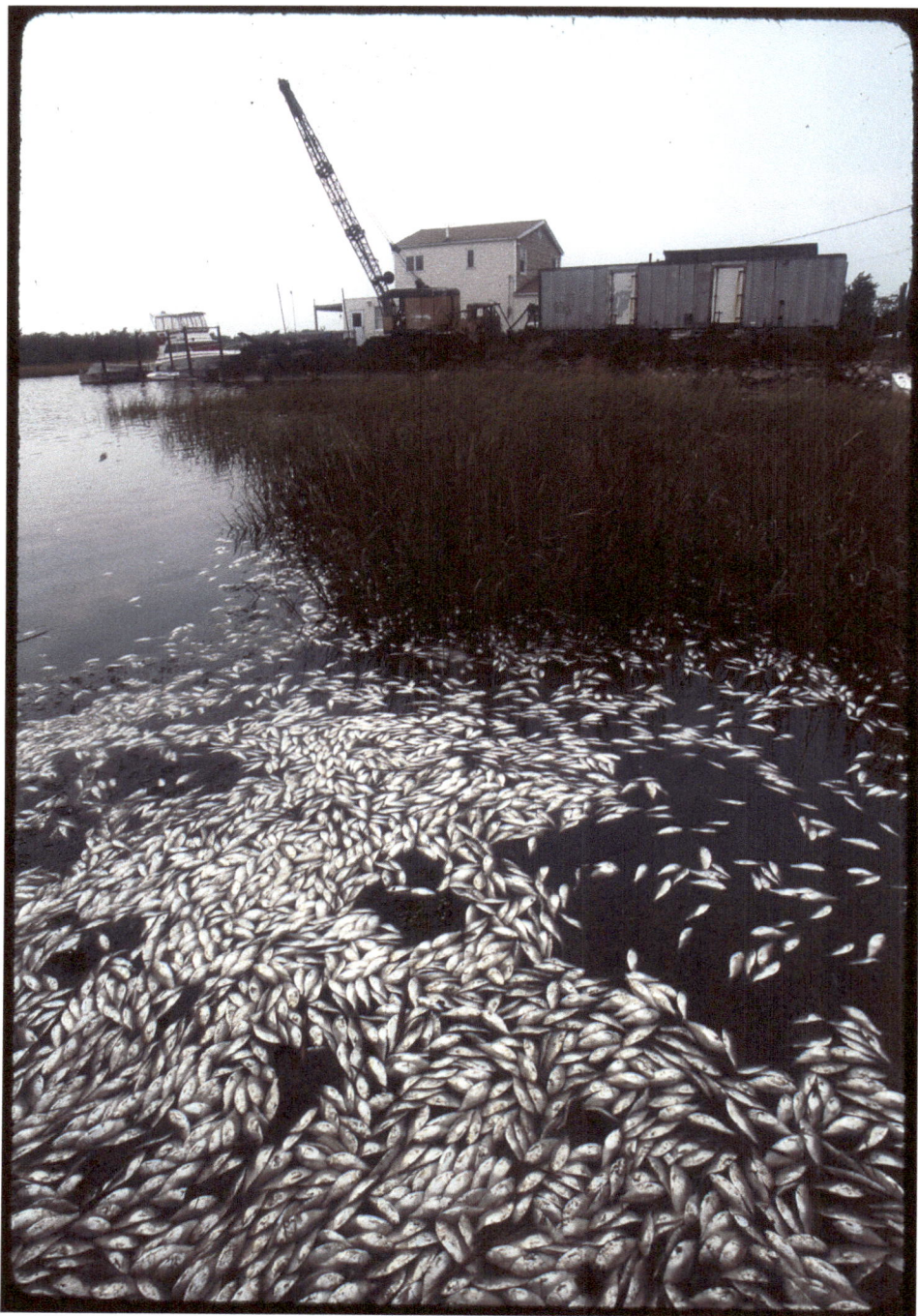

Menhaden fish kill, Broad Channel. c. 1998

Algal bloom, East Pond, Jamaica Bay Wildlife Refuge. c. 1995

Sand spit at Elders Point East, looking south-west. c. 1994

Sand spit at Ruffle Bar Island, looking north-west. c. 1994

"Return-A-Gift Pond," Floyd Bennett Field, looking south-east. c. 1989

Grasslands at Floyd Bennett Field. c. 1990

Breezy Point Surf Club, looking north-east. c. 1994

Breezy Point Tip and Rockaway Point Jetty, Gateway National Recreation Area, looking south-west. c. 1994

Canarsie Pier and Manhattan Skyline, looking north-west. c. 1990

Belt Parkway and Spring Creek, looking north. c. 1990

Gulls feeding on surf clams, Breezy Point Tip, looking south-west.

Fountain Avenue Landfill and Empire State Building. c. 1983

North Channel Bridge, Cross Bay Boulevard (prior to reconstruction), looking south. c. 1986

Subway tracks to Broad Channel, north end of East Pond, looking south-west. c. 1986

Cross Bay Veterans Memorial Bridge and Big Egg Marsh restoration, looking south-east. c. 2003

Rainbow dredging for Big Egg Marsh restoration, looking south towards Rockaway Peninsula. c. 2003

Marsh edge.

Collapse at marsh edge, Jamaica Bay Wildlife Refuge.

JoCo Marsh. c. 1990

Laughing Gull nests at JoCo Marsh. c. 1990

West Pond, Fountain Avenue Landfill and Empire State Building. c. 1987

Don Riepe, American Littoral Society Northeast Chapter Director

Don Riepe founded the Northeast Chapter of the American Littoral Society in 1985 and has been the Society's Jamaica Bay Guardian since 2004. With twenty-five years as a naturalist and manager of the National Park System's Jamaica Bay Wildlife Refuge, Don is a staunch defender of wildlife and habitat in the urban littoral zone. Frequently called upon to testify at hearings on behalf of Jamaica Bay, Don recently made a significant contribution to the passage of legislation to protect New York City's remaining wetlands. In 2010, Don started the Friends of Jamaica Bay Refuge to educate community members about the importance and values of this tidal estuary in New York City. Don's writings and photographs have been published in Scientific American, National Wildlife, Audubon, Defenders, Underwater Naturalist, Parade, and The New York Times. He is a member of the Board of the NYC Audubon Society and the Rockaway Waterfront Alliance, and is a founding member as well as Secretary/Treasurer of the NYC Butterfly Club. He holds a Master of Science in Natural Resource Management from the University of New Hampshire.

All photos in this publication are © Don Riepe and have been reproduced with his permission.

www.ingramcontent.com/pod-product-compliance
Lightning Source LLC
Chambersburg PA
CBHW060826270326
41931CB00002B/77